how to recognize a Good Man

LaKeida M. Belvin-Robertson

Impact|Publishing

Impacting your world with inspiration™

But whatever is good and perfect comes to us from God.

—James 1:17a (TLB)

how to recognize a Good Man

Unless otherwise indicated, Scripture quotations are taken from the Living Bible Version of the Bible.

Scripture quotations marked (TLB) are taken from the *The Living Bible*, copyright © 1971. Used permission of Tyndale House Publishers, Inc., Wheaton, IL 60189. All rights reserved.

The author has emphasized some words in Scripture quotation in bold and italicized type.

ISBN 13: 978-0-578-02206-2
Printed in the United States of America.

Published by:
Impact Publishing, LLC
PO Box 74610
Baton Rouge, LA 70874

Cover/Interior design by:
www.r2design.com

CONTENTS

DEDICATION

First, I dedicate this book to **God** who in his ability has given me the ability to write this book.

Secondly, I dedicate this book to my **GOOD** MAN and husband, **Rodney D. Robertson**. Thank you for your character, relationship with God, integrity, honesty, commitment, and unconditional love for me. They have inspired me to write this book so other women can experience a piece of heaven like I have found in you and in our marriage. You are my partner for life!

I also dedicate this book to my little sister, **Michelle Lewis**. Michelle you are beautiful, smart, intelligent, and priceless. I love you and you are a precious jewel. *Don't settle for anything or any man less than what you are worth!*

SPECIAL THANKS

To my husband, Rodney Robertson, for your generous help, prayers, love and support. I am in love with you always.

To my mother, Carolyn Lewis, if it were not for your unselfish decision to bring me in this world I wouldn't be here. Thanks for loving me and taking care of me. I love you!

To Beverly Robertson and John Robertson Sr., thanks for your many contributions in my life, emotionally, spiritually, and financially. I love you both.

To my brothers, Leslie Lewis Jr., Myron Lewis, and Byron Lewis, thanks for being some of the few GOOD MEN in the world.

To my little sister, Michelle Lewis, for all of your love, respect and for valuing my words of wisdom. I am always here for you and I love you.

To my aunt, Denise, thanks for all of the seeds of love and financial seeds that you and your family have sown in my life. Thanks for always loving me like I was your own.

To my Aunt Kaye and Uncle Marvin Carmouche thanks for all that you have contributed to my life. Thanks for sharing your lives and home!

A special thanks to all those who made special financial contributions:

John Duncan

Monique & Marvin Belvin

The Duncan Family

INTRODUCTION

While I was attending a church service in Zachary, LA, the pastor of the church was teach/preaching a message on being available to God. For those who don't know what teach/preaching is, it is when the minister is equipping you with the knowledge of the Word while exalting you so much you can't stand to sit on your seat any longer. OK, back to the introduction (lol). The man of God was led to elaborate to the young women about a **GOOD** MAN when he read out of Exodus 2:17-21. This passage explained how Moses helped the daughters of the priest of Midian when shepherds tried to run them off while they were trying to draw water for their flock.

Not only did Moses run the shepherds off, which was dangerous, but he watered the flock for the women. He used the authority and power he had within himself as a man to help some women he didn't know. The respect, love, and relationship he gained from the nurture of his mother transferred over to these women. Oh, My God! When the man of God brought this out in the text, the Holy Spirit just leaped within me and this book was conceived.

This book *How to Recognize a **GOOD MAN*** is being birthed out of this powerful message. Prior to this encounter my husband and I were discussing a book God had given him to write called, *How to Keep a **GOOD MAN**,* and I believe these books are a set of twins conceived from God, birthed and delivered by the Holy Spirit. I want to express to every woman whether black, white, Asian, Chinese, rich, or poor that *you don't have to settle for a man unworthy of your EXCELLENCY!*

We as women must learn how to recognize a **GOOD MAN!** You're probably saying to yourself, what makes her an expert on knowing a **GOOD** MAN! Well, I can tell you it isn't a lot of degrees or certificates certifying me to know this. The wisdom I have comes from God first, and then through wisdom I have gained understanding, which comes from life's experiences and the Word of God.

I know this wisdom works and is good because I have a **GOOD** MAN named Rodney D. Robertson. I couldn't have inherited a better man if I had created him myself (lol). So, my life experiences and the Word of God are going to coach you through this process.

First, we should know that **GOD** is the key component to **GOOD**. Without **GOD** in **GOOD**, we find ourselves left with the letter 'O' which means nothing, it is incomplete. This is the result of men without God in their lives; they are left empty and incomplete. Anything good will consist of God because He is a key component of anyone or anything that is truly successful, including men and relationships. A **GOOD** MAN is one who has been influenced by GOD in some degree in his life. Our ability to be **GOOD** comes from **GOD**.

Secondly, in our search for **GOOD** MEN we must first become **GOOD** WOMEN because a man will respond first to what he sees. My husband would often tell me that a man is stimulated first by what he sees. I believe this statement isn't limited to our outer appearance, although it is a part, but it also includes that inner beauty; self-confidence, intelligence, and wholeness that is reflected on the outside.

So, my sisters, get ready to be equipped with the knowledge of *How to Recognize a **GOOD** MAN!*

You will be as much value to
others as you have been
to yourself.

—Marcus Tullius Cicero

Chapter One

Woman of Value

One of the greatest lessons of my life happened when the revelation came to me that *people will treat you the way you treat yourself!* With this revelation, I realized that people also see you the way you see yourself. Whatever we see when we look in a mirror, whether it is a person of poverty or wealth, ignorance or intelligence, success or failure we reflect this image to others who we encounter on a daily basis.

The example that the Holy Spirit revealed to me was simple, but true and powerful. He said think about when you're shopping to buy a gift for someone. The quality of the gift you buy depends on the self worth or value of the person. I am going to use my little sister as an example. When I shop for Michelle, I am cautious because she has a taste of quality. She likes certain brand names and stores; therefore, I wouldn't go to a blue light special and buy her a clothing gift.

Now because of growth, I seek to buy everyone nice, quality gifts. Although, I can recall times in the past where I was shopping for a gift and because I knew the person didn't have high self worth and would take anything; I would get the first decent, cheap gift I could find. *If your value of yourself is poor, then the majority of the things you gain in life will be of poor value, including relationships.*

In a recent *FREE TO BE ME* seminar, my husband, Rodney, made a powerful statement that, *"If we don't know who we are, we don't know what we can do!"* I am going to take it a step further and say *if we don't know who we are, we don't know what we can have!* YES, we can have the best of everything in this world, but first we must know we deserve it. Another statement that my husband expressed in his seminar was that when we have a low opinion of ourselves, it's because we don't know God's true opinion of us. No matter who you are God said that His thoughts toward you are good and not evil. When God finished creating the earth and its components, He said, **"IT'S GOOD."** Whether **IT** is an expensive car, house, job, or husband, you can have **IT** with the revelation of your own immeasurable value.

Knowing Who You Are

For some of you, knowing who you are comes easy because of the solid family structure that you have derived from. You had mothers and fathers who instilled in you self-worth and value. They told you that you can have anything and be anything you put your minds and hearts to. Your parents supported you in every endeavor no matter how time consuming it was.

My husband came up in a family similar to this. He had a family that believed he could be or accomplish anything. When I met him he knew his value, but I didn't know my own value. I didn't know who I was and as a result, I saw his confidence as pride because I didn't possess it.

Many of you may have come from a background like mine. I never had anyone after my grandmother died to affirm me. She loved me unconditionally. When she was living, I felt like a little princess in a magical kingdom even though we lived in a low income neighborhood. My grandmother stayed across the street from my mother, stepfather, and I, so I had unlimited access to her love and attention. She made me feel so important as if I was God's gift to this world. Even though I had an absent father, a stepfather who didn't know I existed most of the time, and a mother so hurt in her marriage she couldn't share the totality of her love with me, while my grandmother was there I was never conscious of it. She died when I was about 8 or 9 years old and this would change my world dramatically.

She wasn't there to affirm me. She wasn't there to make me feel like God's gift any more. After years of disappointments, hurts, abuse (sexual and mental), I began to lose the little princess image I tried so hard to hold on to. I stopped feeling like God's gift and more like His mistake.

After having no one to keep affirming me after my grandmother's death, my self-worth and value depreciated dramatically. There were many times I would ask God, "Why did you put me here?" Not knowing he had a plan for my life all along.

After high school and many unsuccessful relationships, which devalued me even more, I couldn't handle life alone anymore and made a decision to give my life to God.

While living for Him in a church that didn't teach you about who you are in Christ, I still didn't know how much I was worth to God, myself, or others. I began to get a glimpse of my value as I discovered Pastor T.D. Jakes on my little, black and white 13" TV that I would watch every Sunday at 5:00 pm before heading to my own church service. The knowledge I was gaining from the man of God was still being challenged by my past, absent of a father's love, and my present, filled with relationships with fake men in the church.

I then began to seek God for myself and moved to a local ministry teaching the Word. At this time, I also had reconnected with my real father. My self-worth was building and I was finding out my value when God introduced my husband into my life.

Rodney and I ended up getting married and experiencing many difficulties in the beginning of our relationship which challenged once again my self-worth and value. Through this process, God continued to reveal his love to me. It was after my husband and I experienced some hurt, disappointment, and deception in the ministry when I really began to experience the unconditional love of God and recognized all that he had placed in me.

I went through a lot before I realized the price tag that God placed on me that Jesus paid for said PRICELESS! All of the negative relationships I encountered in my life were a result of not knowing who I was and that I was priceless.

Material things don't account for our value as women. Our value as women is determined by our character and the treasures we possess inside. Don't try to conform to who you think a man wants you to be. Be yourself! The treasures that are within you are unique and need to be shared with others. So, no matter what your background is, find out who you are so that when your **GOOD** MAN comes he can experience the real you and not some imitation. *We don't have to pretend to be someone we aren't when the original God created is so magnificent!*

If I were to go to an art gallery, the price tag on the original would be much more expensive than the price tag of a copy. Most of the time, a copy can be purchased in a local store, but for the original you have to go to an art gallery. *You are much more valuable as an original than a cheap copy!* So, as my husband says in his book **FREE TO BE ME**, "Be the You God Created." In order to find out just how precious you are as a woman, go to the **BIBLE**. Even if you have never looked in the Bible before, give it a try. I promise that you will only find essential information to make you a better you. Look in Proverbs 31 and see how precious this woman was that her kids called her blessed. Can you imagine your children telling their friends how blessed and happy they are to have a mother like you and a husband who brags about you to his co-workers and friends? This woman was "bad"! She was a woman of business. She had all kinds of creative abilities. She mastered being a homemaker. This woman had it going on.

There are many women in the Bible whose lives can be an example of womanhood to us and show us our value as women. Proverbs is also an awesome tool for developing our character. No matter what level of affirmation we have had in our lives, sometimes our lives can become tainted by people and events. It is left up to us to discover the unique person God has created us to be.

In order for our value to be priceless, we have to be an original. *Women, in our discovery that we are priceless originals, we will not sell out to the first bidder, but to the highest bidder of MANhood.*

A man should never have the responsibility or privilege of defining who we are as women. That responsibility belongs to us and is granted by God. God desires for us to define our character by His Word, but He has given each of us the freedom to be our own unique selves. *A woman who gives a man the power to define who she is limits her ability to grow and develop into the person God has predestined for her to be.* A man given this type of power will box you into who he desires you to be. He may desire a woman who will stay at home, clean, cook, and take care of his needs and the children. There isn't anything wrong with a man desiring for his wife to do these things, but you may be destined to be the first, female President of the United States of America!

Don't be afraid to be different from the expectation of others, especially a man. It is those differences that define us and complement him.

KEY POINTS

☑ *People will treat you the way you treat yourself.*

☑ *If your value of yourself is poor, then the majority of the things you gain in life will be of poor value, including your relationships.*

☑ *A woman who gives a man the power to define who she is limits her ability to grow and develop into the person God has predestined for her to be.*

☑ *It is our differences that define us and complement him.*

☑ *When you discover that you are a priceless original, you will not sell out to the first bidder, but to the highest bidder of MANhood!*

How to Recognize A GOOD MAN

PERSONAL NOTES:

_____

_____

_____

_____

_____

_____

_____

_____

_____

_____

_____

_____

_____

_____

_____

_____

_____

_____

_____

_____

_____

_____

The secret of living
a life of excellence is merely a
matter of thinking thoughts
of excellence. Really, it's a matter
of programming our minds
with the kind of information
that will set us free.

—Charles R. Swindoll

Chapter Two

Woman of Excellence

I just want you to imagine with me for a moment getting out of a hot, steamy shower and then going to the mirror trying to comb your hair or put on your make-up. We all know we have to wait a few minutes or take a towel and wipe away the steam from the glass or we can't see the complete image that is being reflected.

This is what happens in our judgment as women when we aren't complete within ourselves and we are searching for a **GOOD** MAN. Our ability to see their true person becomes clouded by our own lack of development. *What we don't possess within our own character we can't identify in another's character.* To truly recognize a **GOOD** MAN, we have to be a good woman and be whole within our own person.

A **GOOD** MAN is going to look for a **GOOD** WOMAN; one who knows who she is and is complete within herself. A **GOOD** MAN isn't going to look for a woman divided within herself. A house that is divided will not stand, neither will a woman. I believe most **GOOD** MEN expect to accent us as women, but not build us completely.

Have you ever seen an unattractive woman and then you look on the side of her and holding tightly is this gorgeous man? He is holding on to her as if she is the last woman on earth and every other man is after her. I know! I have seen this situation many times while walking in the mall. I would often ask myself the question, "What does he see in her?" As I got older, I began to realize *he sees everything she sees in herself.* The result of her knowing who she is is him knowing who she is. Even though she may not be the best looking girl in town, he knows she is a priceless original. *Some of the most valuable paintings in this world aren't attractive to the common eye, but to the eye of a trained artist it is extraordinary.* No matter what our outer appearance is we must learn to love who God has created us to be!

Becoming Whole

Imagine again with me, you decided to purchase a manufactured home. You begin the search by going to various manufactured home builders to look at the multiple styles, sizes, and colors of the model homes before making a final decision. OK, now you walk into this one model home and love everything about it, the interior and exterior. Oh, yea! This is definitely the one for you!

You go and do the proper paper work. Now you are just waiting for the day of delivery. You began to purchase the right accents to bring everything in the home together

17

collectively. You receive news that they have delivered your home and you rush from work to begin moving in. When you pull up, Oh! My God! The exterior is even more beautiful than the model home you viewed. However, you open the door, walk inside and you see that the home is gutted. There is only a shell! There are no cabinets, no walls, or any of the interior designs you saw before.

How many of you know that this home would be going back the same day and the home that was ordered brought to the proper place! Imagine the disappointment and the look that would be on your face when receiving the wrong home. This is what happens when we as women are incomplete dating a **GO**OD MAN and he thinks he has a complete woman. He really doesn't know the real you.

From the very first time you met him, you began to perform for him. Not knowing yourself causes you to show and tell him all the things he wants to see and hear. Then one day after catching a glimpse of the real you, the incomplete you, he doesn't call any more or come by. Now you wonder why? It's because as time went by and he began to open the door of your mind and heart; he realized you were incomplete and the job was too big for him. He decided to trade you in for a complete model. One he only had to accent. He wanted a woman, although different from himself, she's already defined. Now his only responsibility is to complement her. The responsibility of completing a person is too big of a job for anyone except God!

Even though the cost of a shell is cheaper, the value of a complete home is more valuable and less time consuming. A complete model is always move in ready and you can add to it your own taste. *Women a man doesn't want to have to put in extra work trying to build the vacant places in your life.* He wants to complement your life and not complete it.

I had to realize this same thing. I had many issues in my life. I thought I was ugly, worthless, too black, and not smart. This load was too heavy for my husband to carry and try to fix. I almost lost him, until I realized I

19

had to get in the presence of God and become whole and complete. I stopped being clingy, jealous, and untrusting. I finally realized that not only had I found a gift in him, but he also found a priceless gift when he found me. The Bible said that when he found me as a wife he found a "**GOOD** THING" and he obtained favor with the Lord. I began to not just feel, but know that I was one of God's gifts to this world.

From that very day, my husband began to see confidence, self-esteem, and trust in my person (the complete me). As a result, our marital relationship and friendship began to grow and develop. I began to blossom on the inside and like a beautiful rose I began to open up. I was developing the inner person to match the beauty on the outside.

Increase your value and worth by not just being a beautiful shell or exterior, but by being the complete package of the beautiful woman God created, internally and externally. Yes my sister, you are one of God's greatest gifts to this world! We are so great that God decided to use one of our bodies to house his most precious Son, Jesus Christ! WOW! I also want to remind you of a woman in the Bible named Mary Magdalene. Mary was caught in the act of adultery and the people wanted to stone her. Mary is then forgiven by Jesus of her sins and he tells her to sin no more. The awesome thing about this story is Mary becomes the one to anoint Jesus for His burial. OK! Women, now God used a virgin woman to bare His Son and a former prostitute to prepare His Son for death. No matter what your past consists of, God sees you as a precious jewel and has created you with a purpose.

Your past doesn't dictate your future! Mary had a past full of mistakes and regrets, but after she met Jesus she realized that she was no longer the same person. She discovered that the price Jesus paid for her made her priceless. Knowing who you are produces a successful future. I am sure that Mary experienced people whispering about her past. *The great thing is no matter how people identified her with her past; Mary proceeded toward her destiny.* When others try to identify you with your past, stay focus and proceed to your destiny as a WOMAN OF EXCELLENCE!

KEY POINTS

☑ *A good man will see everything you see in yourself.*

☑ *A good man doesn't want to put in extra work to build the vacant places in your life.*

☑ *Your past doesn't dictate your future.*

☑ *Even though people may identify you with your past; proceed toward your destiny.*

PERSONAL NOTES:

_____

_____

_____

_____

_____

_____

_____

_____

_____

_____

_____

_____

_____

_____

_____

_____

_____

_____

_____

_____

_____

_____

_____

_____

_____

_____

_____

_____

_____

_____

_____

_____

_____

_____

_____

_____

_____

_____

_____

_____

_____

_____

_____

_____

_____

_____

*Try not to become a man
of success, but rather try to become
a man of value.*

—ALBERT EINSTEIN

Chapter Three

Man of Value

*L*adies, you must take the time to find out the true value of a man before becoming too involved. *Sometimes as women we become intimate emotionally with a man before we find out who he really is.* This is due to the fact that we are created to be emotional beings. *As women, we tend to create the perfect man in our imagination which causes us to apply it to every man we date blinding us to the reality of his true person.*

Sometimes we are blinded for a day, week, month, years, and for some poor women a life time. When looking for a **GO**O**D** MAN, we must learn to keep a magnifying glass in our hands at all times. Make sure the glass is clean and clear. A magnifying glass is used to enlarge objects that are small to the human eye.

When we use a magnifying glass to view potential **GO**O**D** MEN, not just the good is magnified but the impurities also. Don't get me wrong *a **GOOD** MAN isn't a perfect man;* he is a man reaching toward perfection. He constantly seeks to improve his person so that he can be the best he can be. So, don't use the magnifying glass to look for perfection, but to see if the costly material out ways the impurities.

If we were to find a rock with chucks of pure gold imbedded in it, we wouldn't throw away the whole rock. We would extract the gold and throw away the impurities. A **GO**O**D** MAN may have some impurities, but the value of his treasures far out way his impurities. A **GO**o**D** MAN knows who he is!

My husband knew who he was and had so much confidence in himself that I and many others thought he was arrogant. I, myself, never experienced a person with that much confidence and assurance like he possessed. I couldn't see this as a positive attribute because I myself didn't possess it. I can assure you now this is a positive attribute! ***If a man doesn't know who he is, then he will never know where he is going.*** This will result in a lack of direction for his life and yours if you connect with him.

Knowing Who He Is

I was told and over heard many times as I was growing up, "You can tell a lot about a man by the way he treats his mother." Women let me tell you this is so true. Before I ever went on the first date with my husband, I would here about the many things he did for his mother and the great relationship he had with her. He would buy for their home and for her personally. I was told that if Beverly Robertson wanted anything Rodney would go out of his way to get it for her.

CHAPTER THREE *Man of Value*

Some people saw their connection as a negative and tried to poison me against their relationship. My view was if he can do all this for his mother and have this kind of relationship with her; I can imagine what he will do for his wife. After we dated and he proposed, I realized I was that blessed woman. I even had people tell me before our first date that I shouldn't want him because he was a "momma's boy," but something within me just didn't agree with that.

Ladies, I was so right! My husband is so wonderful to me. We have had to face many financial difficulties, but even in the midst, he would find ways to give me gifts and show me he was thinking about me. He even came up with a "Sweetie's Day" for us. On the 29th of each month, we celebrate another month of marriage with giving small gifts to one another. The other day he came in the house with a bundle of various yellow flowers including roses. One of his aunts was at the house when he brought them to me and I over heard here ask my sister-in-law, "Is it their anniversary?" She responded, "No, I guess it is just because." Guess What? It was just because.

The treatment he extended toward his mom has magnified in our relationship. Today, he still does for his mother and I have never tried to stop him from doing so. He has also taught me the same principle with my mom. You may be saying to yourself, what if he doesn't have his mom in his life? If he doesn't, here are some other things to consider:

If his mother has passed away...

Inquire about the relationship he had with her. When he is around other siblings or family and they engage in conversation about his mother pay attention to his reaction and comments.

If his mother was or is an absent mother...

Ask him how he feels about her and watch his reaction. Ask him has he forgiven his mother. Also, pay attention to his treatment of other females in his life, such as sisters, aunts, etc. Notice his conversation toward women. Is he hostile or does he like control and domination? You can also watch just his basic daily conversation and actions. Is he honest when confronted with difficult situations? Believe me there are always tell, tell signs.

If you are an older woman with older children…

You meet a man who shows little or no interest in your children, family or friends, and he shows no sign of wanting you to get involved with his family or friends, RED FLAG. This is a sign of no commitment. He doesn't want to get too attached and he doesn't want you too attached to his life.

If he is divorced…

My husband gives the advice that you should inquire about his failed marriage not only from him, but hold on to your seats, also from the ex-wife. I know there are some women who aren't willing to talk with the girlfriend of their ex-husband. However, there are some ex-wives who aren't bitter, but better and won't mind sharing with you concerning her past marriage with your potential husband. Especially if she still has a good friendship with her ex-husband. Find out why their marriage didn't make it. Remember there are always two sides to a story. You have only heard his side. If you can get both sides of the story, get it! Don't be afraid to ask him questions. Was he abusive in any way, did he have an affair (if so what led to it), and did he provide financially?

If he has children...

Pay attention to his relationship with his children. Is he a "dead beat" dad or is he there for his children? Is he really fathering

35

his children or just being "The Bank of Fatherhood?" Some men provide financially for their children, but spend no time fathering them. Women don't be foolish and celebrate the fact that he may have children, but they aren't in his life! It doesn't matter how old or young his children are he should still have a productive relationship with them. If he isn't there for his present children, what makes you think he will be there for your children if you were to marry him and then for some reason you got divorced? I know of a man right now who has followed the same pattern in each of his relationships. As long as he and the mother are together, he is a great father to his children. As soon as the relationship is over so is his relationship with his children. He has children for various women and he only has a relationship with the child whose mother he is with now. I believe if they were to separate the same would result for this child.

If he doesn't respect your values…

Single women of God, you should be living a life of celibacy; some of you may have fallen. It will be OK! You can get up again, learn the lesson, get cleansed and don't fall again. I heard a saying that, "If you learn the lesson, then you have not failed the test!" Whether it is celibacy, honesty, or integrity don't allow a man to influence you to compromise your values. If he tries to cause you to compromise, GET OUT THE MAGNIFYING GLASS and take a second look, a BIG RED FLAG is waving! Now if you are the one with the wrong values and he challenges you to change, you have discovered a potentially **GOOD** MAN.

If he is committed in a relationship or married…

Whatever! Don't look at me with that tone of voice! Yes, it is happening and a lot of us are the cause. Oh, my sisters, this irritates me so much! I hate to see women manipulated. Let go of the ignorance! First of all, if this is the case, I can tell you there is no commitment and there will be no commitment. You are his new spring, summer, winter, fall or all year round toy. I know a young woman who was compromising herself by remaining in a relationship with a man she dated in the past who is now living with another woman. Her perception was that the other woman is at a disadvantage and is the FOOL! Unfortunately, this young woman died a short time ago and never had the chance to experience the enjoyment of a **GOOD** MAN! Even though she compromised her future and her body, her life wasn't taken by a sexual disease. However, diseases are real! We have to wake up, AIDS isn't something you can just get a towel and wipe off. It is a life-time disease and a short life, unless God heals you. A lot of us have this ignorant idea that as long as he comes home or he keeps coming back to me then you are the BOMB! You are right—a bomb ticking that's about to blow up with some type of disease. Don't compromise your body, soul, or spirit! There are men out there who count on women being this foolish. Know who you are! ***Know that what you have to offer is priceless and it is worth waiting for***. Have respect for yourself and other women. One of the statements I live by now and in high school was, "If he does it to another female, then he will do it to me." I wasn't naive enough to think that I had some type of superwoman power to keep him from returning the same disfavor I would have inflicted on his previous girlfriend.

For those of you dating some woman's husband, as the saying goes, "What goes around comes around." The Bible says it even better, "Whatever seeds we sow (negative or positive), the harvest will come." This was something I lived by even as a teenager. I had at least two married men and several "committed" men who tried to get with me. I shut them down quick! I knew the Bible was true and I would one day be in a serious relationship and get married. I put myself in the other woman's shoes and decided early in life that I didn't want to reap that type of hurt and pain. *The harvest is always greater than the seed planted!*

If you are a younger woman…

One of the things the preacher said in his message was that the priest of the Midians invited Moses to come to their house and eat with them. Moses accepted the offer and dined with them. If you are dating a young man and he doesn't want to meet your family, spend anytime around them, or get to know them, this should be a big RED FLAG going up! If he only wants to take you to a fast food drive-thru at night, RED FLAG! If he only wants to be alone with you and not meet your friends or do just basic daily tasks with you from time to time—another RED FLAG. He has a hidden agenda and it isn't one of commitment.

We must not only be willing to recognize the RED FLAGS, but respond to them in the proper manner. Ask him many questions! Ask others who know him about the real him. If we were to see multiple stop signs and continued to proceed ahead without stopping and checking for traffic, eventually we would end up in an accident which could result in a terrible fatality. This is what happens when we ignore the RED FLAGS that are waving in our faces when we are in unproductive relationships with men who aren't GOOD. Our lives become infected with mental, emotional and sometimes physical abuse, which is fatal to us as a person.

A young woman I know, lets call her Destiny, dated a young man. When her family asked to meet him, he declined the invitation. He would never go by her mom's house. When she told me, I began to wonder what the problem was. I even asked Destiny, "Does he have something to hide? Why doesn't he want to meet your family?" To me that was a tell, tell, sign of no commitment letting me know he was trying to use her.

As time went on, Destiny had to move in with her mom because of financial difficulties. He began to come to her mom's house after she moved in. He still never spent quality time with her or her family, RED FLAG! As time went on she became pregnant. This young man did only those things he was required to do. Destiny is a beautiful, smart, and intelligent young woman who can do anything she puts her mind to. I believe her self-image had been clouded by an absent father and multiple bad relationships. Fortunately, she finally got the strength to call the relationship off!

So my young sisters, if the young man you are involved with doesn't want any part of your family, he doesn't want any part of you. Your family is a part of who you are. If he doesn't want you to meet his family, RED FLAG! This was another issue with this young man. Destiny visited his family's business often and he never introduced her to his parents. To this day even after being pregnant and having the baby, neither she nor the baby has ever been properly introduced to his parents.

This is one of the reasons I felt impressed to write this book, I don't want anyone to go through the terrible relationships Destiny and I have gone through. I can remember myself dating a young man who was much older than I, but we never did anything together outside of drinking, partying, and having sex. For two and a half years, this was all we did. He never took me to a movie, shopping, or out to dinner, but because my self-esteem was so low I thought I had something great—clouded judgment! I felt as long as he was interested in me physically, then, "It was all GOOD." It wasn't all GOOD! It only added to my list of hurts, disappointments, and pains. In the end, he left me for another woman.

I wasn't complete and didn't know my own value, so I settled for what I thought was GOOD! When you see a man who knows who he is and wants to get to know the complete you, your family and friends included, you have definitely found a potentially **GOOD MAN!**

KEY TOPICS

☑ *We as women tend to create the perfect man in our imagination which causes us to apply it to every man we date blinding us to the reality of his true person.*

☑ *A good man is not a perfect man.*

☑ *If a man doesn't know who he is, then he will never know where he is going!*

PERSONAL NOTES:

_____

_____

_____

_____

_____

_____

_____

_____

_____

_____

_____

_____

_____

_____

_____

_____

_____

_____

_____

_____

_____

_____

_____

How to Recognize A Good Man

_____

_____

_____

_____

_____

_____

_____

_____

_____

_____

_____

_____

_____

_____

_____

_____

_____

_____

_____

_____

Excellence is the gradual result of always striving to do better.

—PAT RILEY

Chapter Four

Man of Excellence

A man of excellence is one who is honest, integral, and whole. As I explained in the previous chapter WOMAN OF EXCELLENCE, we must be whole in order to produce successful relationships and marriages. Two halves don't make a whole when it comes to relationships because there will always be a divider between the two. Most of the time, it is a wall of defense not allowing the other spouse to get too close. This wall of separation prevents trust, intimacy and quality communication from existing in the relationship.

Sometimes we enter relationships with the assumption that the other person is supposed to complete us. It is God who completes us, not a man. Our spouse is there to complement us and our destiny. They are there to add to our lives. The only way to add to someone else is to have more than enough to give of yourself. If a man isn't whole then there is not enough of himself to share with you or anybody else. However, a man that is whole will hold nothing back when sharing himself with the woman he loves and is committed to.

A man who is complete within himself isn't afraid to let you in his heart. My husband also told me that a man can give you his body easily, but not his heart. A man has to trust you in order to expose his heart to you. He can only trust you if he isn't fragmented. In order to have a successful relationship or marriage, you both have to give to each other completely. Incompleteness can result in distrust, jealousy, anger, and sometimes abuse. There must be a merging of two complete individuals into a whole unit. A great example of this type of relationship happens when two great companies merge together for a greater good. Both companies have its strengths and weaknesses but they both support one another. No one company carries all of the responsibility of causing the business to succeed. They both contribute what they have for the company's success. They may have begun as two separate companies, but now they become one whole unit working together.

Is He Whole?

An incomplete man is similar to a chair with a weak leg. Meaning, you never know when it is going to give out. He can only support you for a short period of time. Sooner or later, he is going to look for you to fix him. When we have a chair with a weak leg, we can either try and fix it or order a whole new chair from the manufacturer. If you choose to fix it, it is only going to hold for a certain period of time.

You will periodically have to go and apply more glue to keep it together.

On the other hand, if you order a new chair, you wouldn't have to repair it at all. Just enjoy it knowing that it has the ability to support you. A lot of us see the incompleteness of a man and figure we will go ahead take him and fix him. We think all he needs is a little love, attention, and support. Just like tape or glue on a broken chair leg, it may last for a little while, but sooner or later it will become weak again. We will be required to periodically apply more glue just like we will be required to give him whatever it takes to temporarily hold him together. If his weakness is unfaithfulness and you experiment with the type of sex he likes frequently, it may sustain him a little while. However, there will always be a weak spot. If temptation becomes too much weight or pressure for him, he will give out.

I heard Sister Serita Jakes say on a program that if your husband is a scalawag now, then you had to know he was one before you married him. Don't try to act surprised when you see those negative character traits creeping out. You knew they were there before you were married. We as women don't have the tools or power to fix our spouses. God is the only one able to complete a man. We are only responsible for complementing him.

When a man is whole within himself, know matter what kind of pressure he faces, he will endure like a good soldier fully equipped. I can remember a point in my life when the Holy Spirit allowed me to discern a female who was trying to come on to my husband. I didn't get upset or become suspicious of him. I knew who he was and more importantly I knew he knew who he was. I immediately began to watch and pray. Yes, I watched her while I was praying (smile)! I knew this thing was strong because I could feel the spirit of lust when I was around her. I watched her when she was in my husband's company. I never approached the woman. I just continued to pray. I mentioned it to my husband, but he thought I was nuts at that time. Nevertheless, I continued to pray.

One day in particular when he left to go by their house to speak with her husband, I felt the unction to really pray. I wondered why my husband came back home so quickly. A little while later, my husband revealed to me that when he went over to their house her husband wasn't home and this female tried to come on to him very strongly. He said that he quickly got out of her presence and came home. Even after this event she continued her flirting tactics. If my husband would have had a weak spot, he could have given out under that pressure. Thank God for a **GOOD, WHOLE MAN!**

Believe me you want a man that is able to stand the pressure whether he has to stand alone or with you. There were many other situations where my husband and I had to stand under some intense pressure together. Throughout all of the hurts, pains, disappointments, and deceit we endured, Rodney never left me to carry the burden alone. *I can depend on him to bare me up when I need him because he can support the weight of my weaknesses.* A man who wasn't whole couldn't have held up under the pressure Rodney and I endured.

I have seen where people have one chair at there table with a weak leg and they stick it in the corner so no one will sit in it because they fear that it will give out from under them. I have seen people in relationships do the same thing. They don't bring their spouse to certain events or family functions because they fear they will either flirt with other women, get drunk, or verbally abuse them. Why keep a chair in your house that you can't use when you can purchase a new one? Why invest in a man who you won't be able to count on, when you can have a **GOOD MAN**? Before you proceed in a relationship, recognize the weaknesses of the individual. See if those weaknesses have caused him to be fragmented. If he is fragmented, no one can put him back together, but God!

KEY TOPICS

☑ *A man has to trust you in order to expose his heart to you.*

☑ *We don't have the tools or power to fix a man.*

☑ *Don't ignore the weaknesses of a man, recognize and consider them.*

PERSONAL NOTES:

_____

_____

_____

_____

_____

_____

_____

_____

_____

_____

_____

_____

_____

_____

_____

_____

_____

_____

_____

_____

_____

_____

Chapter Four *Man of Excellence*

_____

_____

_____

_____

_____

_____

_____

_____

_____

_____

_____

_____

_____

_____

_____

_____

_____

_____

_____

_____

_____

Destiny is no matter of chance.
It is a matter of choice.
It is not a thing to be waited for;
it is a thing to be achieved.

—WILLIAM JENNINGS BRYAN

Chapter Five

Destiny's Choice

bishop on television was ministering one day and he began to talk about the process in choosing a life-long mate. The summary I received from his message was that our choice should not be determined by outer beauty, money, or convenience, but based on destiny. Is this individual connected to and a part of your destiny? They may be able to accompany you where you are located now, but can they be a productive partner for where your future is taking you? Not everyone is connected to your destiny and you aren't connected to everyone's destiny. If a man's destiny consists of him being a Pastor then the woman that is connected to his destiny by God will have a mothering spirit and leadership abilities.

People often times choose a spouse based on various things. Familiarity is a large reason people stay in unproductive relationships. They fear the unknown. Even though the known may be physical, mental, or emotional abuse, they still choose to stay there because that's all they know. They are familiar with that type of relationship. Others choose to stay in unproductive relationships out of obligation. They feel like they need to be with their "Baby's Daddy" because they share a child together. Just because you share a child with someone doesn't mean you need to share a life time of a marriage filled with heartache and pain. The only obligation and connection you have for a life time is your child and to be good parents. ***Your connection to your spouse should never be because of feelings or***

material things but because of your destiny. Feelings and material things can and sometimes do fade with time. Choose life that you and your seed my live so that your hopes, dreams, and visions my live. ***Choose destiny, not convenience***!

When I began dating my husband, I began to see his vision for his life and how I could see myself being a productive part. I could see him connected to my destiny and the fulfillment of God's purpose for my life. My husband is an essential part of my destiny. The vision for my own personal life has grown tremendously because of his vision for us. Destiny's choice will promote the vision in us and not kill it! In him, I can see me. When I look at him or his life, I am not lost in it but I am a active partner in it. We have become two complete individuals merged into one awesome unit. This is only possible when you find destiny within one another. Our destiny's have met and intertwined with one another to produce the will of God for our lives.

Is He a Part of Your Destiny?

Have you noticed how many couples are getting divorced? Most of these couples are Christians who have been together for many years, and have decided they no longer wanted to be together. There are about four couples that have separated or divorced in the church I grew up in. These couples have been together for years, worshipped together, and raised children together, yet it wasn't enough to keep them together. What is the problem? I believe they never found or saw destiny in one another. Just think about it, what if you could see a video of your future? In the video you see a certain man that is an essential part of your purpose and destiny. This man is going to be the one who causes you to succeed in life and help you to become a millionaire. How quick would you let him go when challenges present themselves?

My husband and I went through some difficult challenges and encountered some people who almost destroyed our marriage, but no matter how hard things got I was connected to him and he to me. We didn't let go of each other. He was my DESTINY'S CHOICE ordained by God. *Many men came and left, but he was the only one anointed to stay!*

As a woman desiring a GoOD MAN, you may be wondering how you can identify or recognize destiny's choice. There are many ways to identify a man of destiny. A man of destiny possesses certain character traits. These special traits can aid us in determining if the man we have in our life is our man of destiny. So right now, I want to provide you with a special checklist to help you determine if the man in your life is a part of your destiny, is he your GOoD Man!

A Man of Destiny

A man of destiny has the ability to bring out of you potential you didn't even know existed within you:

He is able to look at you and go beyond the external of your being. He is able to see the internal part of you that you keep hidden from

69

the rest of the world because you are afraid of rejection. He embraces this part of you and encourages you to share it with others. I knew I had many creative abilities before I met my husband. I could do hair designs, multiple crafts, and even write poems, but I never saw myself being successful in any of these fields until Rodney revealed my potential to me. No matter what talents I discovered within myself, I minimized them, while my husband maximized them. He could see me greater than I could see myself. He encouraged me to stir up the gifts that God has placed with in me. *You are going to need a **GOOD** MAN who can remind you of your destiny even when it seems blurry to you.*

A man of destiny promotes your future, purpose, and vision:

He is never intimidated by any talent or gifting you may have. He is your personal cheering squad. He believes in you regardless of your mistakes and failures because he sees your end not just your beginning. My husband even maximized my gifts when others minimized them. I remember one time in particular when I decided I would like to go to cosmetology school so I could finally do something I enjoyed. I have enjoyed doing hair since I was a little girl. I remember burning my Barbie's hair because I was experimenting with it (lol). I mentioned my decision to go to cosmetology school to someone whose opinion at the time I trusted above my own and my husband's. This person told me I was better than being a hair stylist. His comment degraded my gift. After listening to him, I felt like if I followed that dream I would be worthless. So at first, I decided not to pursue it; however, until my husband continued to remind me of the

71

greatness of my gift. Rodney continued to feed my soul with encouragement and confidence to know that I had a special gift for cosmetology and that I would be successful. So, I have made the decision to still pursue cosmetology and add it to my list of many accomplishments. He continued to promote my future and destiny even when I didn't see clearly enough to promote them myself.

A man of destiny is a vision of safety:

He represents every thing we identify as strong. He has the ability to send us back in time becoming that innocent little girl with no worries in the world. His arms represent safety because we know he has our best interest in mind. We can feel secure in his love for us because we know he is faithful and committed. When we have secure locks on the doors and windows of our homes, we can rest at night feeling safe and secure. This same safety is represented in our man of destiny. His love for us makes us feel so safe and secure that we can rest knowing that every thing inside of us is protected from harm and danger. *Our health is protected by his faithfulness and our heart is protected by his commitment to us.* You can always rest in the love of your DESTINY'S CHOICE!

In my opinion, the perfect example of a DESTINY'S CHOICE mistake is that of a famous female singer; we will call her Star. I know most of us are familiar with Star and her career. I remember as a little girl wishing I could sing like her. Most little girls at that time fantasized about being Star. Star's songs reached a variety of people. The older she became the more beautiful and talented she became, until she met her boyfriend and we will call him Tyrone. I recently viewed a television series they did on her where she went to a foreign country to be baptized and get her life together. I remember while I was watching the show that my heart went out to her. I also told my family members watching with me that her life began to deteriorate when she married Tyrone.

Tyrone wasn't her DESTINY'S CHOICE. He destroyed her destiny instead of promoting it! Since she has connected with him, only one good thing has come out of their relationship and that is her beautiful daughter. Her life has been steadily decreasing. Her voice is deteriorating and she looks old, tired, worn-out, and unhealthy. Star was at the peak of her career when she married Tyrone. I believe she would have remained at that peak for many years and become the next Aretha Franklin for our generation if she had not married Tyrone. Instead of contributing to her down fall, if Tyrone was DESTINY'S CHOICE, he would have contributed to making her life even more of a success. He would have contributed to Star becoming a better person. Star may be on the road to recovery now. I pray that she is. ***Women our choices in our spouse today***

can determine our success or failure tomorrow! So, know who you are, become whole, know who he is, and make a DESTINY'S CHOICE!

KEY TOPICS

- ☑ *A man of destiny will bring out potential you didn't know existed within you.*
- ☑ *A man of destiny promotes your future, purpose, and vision.*
- ☑ *A man of destiny is a vision of safety.*
- ☑ *Some men may come and go, but there is only one anointed to stay!*
- ☑ *A man of destiny protects your health by his faithfulness and your heart by his commitment to you.*
- ☑ *The choice of your spouse today will determine your success or failure tomorrow!*

PERSONAL NOTES:

_____

_____

_____

_____

_____

_____

_____

_____

_____

_____

_____

_____

_____

_____

_____

_____

_____

_____

_____

_____

_____

_____

_____

_____

_____

_____

_____

_____

_____

_____

_____

_____

_____

_____

_____

_____

_____

_____

_____

_____

_____

_____

_____

SELF EXAMINATION

Change is only achievable when we recognize where we are located and apply what we've learned. What are 3 things that you have learned from this book and 3 ways you will apply them?

Things Learned:

1. _____
_____
_____
_____
_____
_____
_____
_____

2. _____
   _____
   _____
   _____
   _____
   _____
   _____
   _____
   _____

3. _____
   _____
   _____
   _____
   _____
   _____
   _____
   _____
   _____

How to Apply:

1. _____
   _____
   _____

How to Recognize A GOOD MAN

_____

_____

_____

_____

_____

_____

2. _____

_____

_____

_____

_____

_____

_____

_____

3. _____

_____

_____

_____

_____

_____

_____

_____

_____

ABOUT THE AUTHOR

LaKeida M. Belvin-Robertson is the founder and CEO of Daughters of Destiny International. She is a highly respected teacher, mentor, speaker, and minister. She is also a relationship coach, author, and entrepreneur.

Her mission is to equip and empower people with the wisdom of God to live successful lives. She is the co-founder of New Life Christian Center and is married to her partner for life, Rodney D. Robertson. They reside in Louisiana.

A PRAYER
FOR GODLY WISDOM

The first step to godly wisdom is to be committed to Christ Jesus. If you have not given Him your life, then your life isn't in His control. Jesus doesn't take from us anything we don't want to freely give. He doesn't give to us anything we don't want to freely receive. Our Father has allowed His Son Christ Jesus to give to us eternal life, salvation, and the Holy Spirit. All we have to do is acknowledge Him as Lord over our spirit, soul, and body. The benefits of God only come when we commit to Him just like benefits on our job only come when we commit to it.

So, if you are ready to commit your life and receive wisdom from God not only for relationships but every area of your life then repeat this prayer:

Father, I come to you in your Son, Christ Jesus name. I ask you to forgive me of all my sins. I acknowledge that your Son, Christ Jesus was born, died, and was resurrected so that I could be set free from the law of sin and death. Today I confess Jesus as Lord over my life and I ask that you would send your Holy Spirit to fill me. From this day on my life is committed to You. In Jesus name, Amen!

Now that you have become apart of the Body of Christ, you are heir to God's promises. God tells us in his Word that he stores up godly Wisdom for us and that all we have to do is ask. So, now follow me in prayer as we ask for His Wisdom.

Father, in Jesus name we pray and ask that you will grant us your godly Wisdom. We ask that your Wisdom will increase in our lives daily so that we are able to make decisions of destiny. We thank You for giving us your Wisdom. She

86

will lead us and guide us to our destiny in you.
You said to only ask and you will give us Wisdom.
So, we receive Wisdom as our daily companion
in life. In Jesus name, Amen.

SPECIAL REQUEST

I appreciate and am very grateful to every individual who sowed into my life and their own by purchasing this book. I pray that this book has been a blessing to you. I pray that it has been an eye opening and life changing experience. If this book, *How to Recognize a* **GOOD** *MAN* has blessed you the way it blessed me just by writing it, buy it for a friend, co-worker, sister, or cousin who you know is in desperate need of relationship counseling or for a single woman needing wisdom in choosing a spouse. Thank you.

TO CONTACT
THE AUTHOR:

Address: LaKeida M. Robertson

PO Box 74610

Baton Rouge, LA 70874

E-mail: ladylrobertson@ymail.com

Online: www.rodneyrobertson.org

OTHER BOOKS

BY IMPACT PUBLISHING, LLC

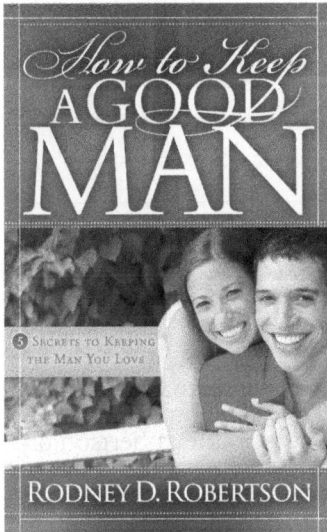

ISBN: 9780615186986

A good man is hard to find. In this day and time, a
good man is a rare commodity. Inside this best seller, you

will discover the secrets to keeping a good man without the help of tricks, schemes, games, and love potions.

You will discover love solutions that will reveal what a good man wants and how you can keep him. If you're already married, your love skills will be sharpened. If you're a lady in waiting, you will be equipped with meaningful insights for the good man that is on the way. *Get ready to enjoy more of life, love, and a lasting connection with your good man.*

Available online at:

www.amazon.com

www.rodneyrobertson.org

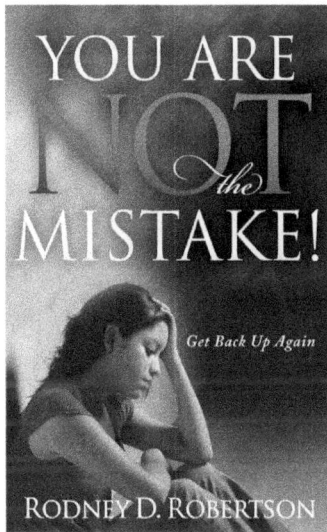

ISBN: 9780615261959

You are not the mistake you made! Inside this life changing book, Rodney will show you how to make a comeback from the place where you've fallen. Through his message of hope and restoration, you will find out that God still loves you, he stands ready to forgive you and you can get up again.

Inside *You are Not the Mistake*, you will learn things like:

- *How to find life after the mistake,*
- *How to forget it and move on,*

- *How to worship your way to wholeness,*
- *How to get free from the guilt of the past and so MUCH MORE.*

It is your time to get up and walk in your destiny. It doesn't matter if you have fallen one time or 101 times. You aren't what you did. Though a just man falls seven times, he will arise again (Proverbs 24:16). Get ready to receive God's forgiveness, healing, the power to forgive yourself, and the strength to walk in victory every day. **You are Not the Mistake!**

Available online at:

www.amazon.com

www.rodneyrobertson.org

www.ingramcontent.com/pod-product-compliance
Lightning Source LLC
Chambersburg PA
CBHW060117050426
42448CB00010B/1917